# Praying from the Cave

---

*Finding God in the Dark*

**Lynne Free**

# Table of Contents

# Dedication

*To those who seek God in the shadows and find strength*

*in the struggle.*

# About the Author

Lynne is the passionate host of the podcast *'Real Life with Lynne,'* where she explores the intersection of faith and real-life struggles. As a devoted disciple of Jesus and a non-profit leader, Lynne has navigated personal valleys, including battles with depression and the challenges of divorce. Through her experiences, she has cultivated a deep understanding of hope and resilience in dark times. Lynne shares her journey with the heartfelt desire to impact others, offering them a beacon of light and encouragement. Her writing aims to remind readers that even in the most profound shadows, there is always a glimmer of hope.

# Introduction

Life often leads you into dark, desolate caves, where hope seems distant and the walls close in around you. In these moments, you feel alone, abandoned, and desperate for a way out. As a Christian, you turn to the Bible for comfort, finding solace in the stories of those who have walked this path before you. One such story is that of David, who, though anointed as king, found himself hiding in a cave, fearing for his life. In this place of despair, he penned Psalm 142, a heartfelt cry to God.

David's cave is a powerful metaphor for the emotional and spiritual caves you encounter. Whether wrestling with depression, anxiety, or life's pressures, the cave represents those seasons when you feel trapped and forsaken. Yet, in these moments, prayer can become your lifeline, connecting you with God and leading you back to the light.

Psalm 142 offers a raw and honest example of how to pray from a cave. David's words are a direct and urgent plea for God's intervention, and a reminder to you that it is okay to be vulnerable with God, to express your deepest fears and frustrations. In doing so, you open yourself to His comfort and guidance.

This book is a guide for you, a Christian in the cave of depression and despair. Drawing from David's example in Psalm 142, we will explore how to cultivate a prayer life that is honest, persistent, and rooted in faith. Each chapter offers practical steps and spiritual insights to help you navigate your own cave experience.

In these pages, you will find spiritual wisdom, practical questions to deepen your prayer life, and reflections on God's faithfulness. Whether you are in the midst of a cave season or seeking to support someone who is, this book is a companion for your journey. Together, we will discover that even in the darkest of caves, God's light can shine through, bringing healing, hope, and renewed purpose.

As we embark on this journey, remember that you are not alone. God is with you in the cave, listening to your cries and guiding your steps. With each prayer, you draw closer to Him, finding strength in His presence and assurance in His love. May this book encourage you and remind you that no matter how deep the cave is, God's light is always within reach.

# Living Life from the Cave: My Story

I've been a Christian for most of my life, and I know firsthand how it feels to wrestle with the darkness of depression. It's a battle that seems never-ending, and sometimes it feels like there's no way out. In college, things were particularly tough for me. I was either sleeping too much or not enough, eating too little or too much, and trying to self-medicate with classes, caffeine, and endless screen time. Eventually, I turned to medication for a few years to help me navigate through the darkness.

At first, the medication helped me avoid the deep discouragement, but it also numbed me to joy. I wasn't feeling deeply discouraged, but I wasn't feeling joy either. After a while, with regular medical check-ins, I decided to taper off the medication and focus on developing healthy coping mechanisms and seeing a counselor.

It hasn't been a perfect journey. There were weekends when I binge-watched Netflix or Hulu, convincing myself I was "resting" when I was really just escaping. But God has helped me become more aware of patterns in myself that signal something is wrong.

Wearing the same t-shirt 2-3 times in a work week, a messy kitchen, or not enjoying hobbies like playing guitar or painting—these are red flags for me.

Some days, I let myself feel my feelings and remind myself of the truth, and the emotion passes. Other days are harder, and I linger in the cave a little longer. But my life is a living testimony of how God can help someone prone to depression truly live, even in the darkest moments. And I am fully convinced that He can help you, too, no matter what internal or external cave you're in.

When I was at my lowest, I clung to God's promises. It took time, but I learned that it was okay to be honest with Him about my struggles and to lean on the support of my faith community. Reflecting on His goodness, even in small ways, became a lifeline. God's faithfulness didn't always pull me out of the cave immediately, but it gave me the strength to keep moving forward, one step at a time.

Developing healthy coping mechanisms has been crucial. Regular exercise, a balanced diet, and consistent sleep have helped stabilize my mood. Engaging in hobbies and connecting with friends and family provide joy and support. Seeing a counselor has offered me a safe space to process my feelings and gain valuable insights.

I've also learned the importance of recognizing warning signs and addressing them early. When I notice myself slipping into old patterns, I take proactive steps to care for my mental health. This might mean taking a break, seeking additional support, or adjusting my routine. It's a continuous process of self-awareness and adaptation.

God's grace has been a constant companion on this journey. He has met me in my darkest moments, offering comfort and hope. His presence reminds me that I am not alone, even when the cave feels all-encompassing. Through prayer, Scripture, and worship, I find strength and encouragement to persevere.

Living life from the cave isn't about never experiencing darkness; it's about finding light and hope in the midst of it. God's faithfulness has taught me that even in the darkest seasons, there is a way forward. By leaning on Him and the support of others, you can navigate your own caves and discover the abundant life He offers.

This book comes was born out of my own struggles with depression and the darkness of life's caves. The practical steps and insights I share are not just theoretical but are things I practice today. From developing healthy coping mechanisms to leaning on God's promises, every chapter reflects what I've found to be essential in my walk with Him.

My story, woven throughout these pages, is a testament to the transformative power of honest prayer, community support, and unwavering faith in God's goodness. He has helped me through my struggles, and I believe He can do the same for you. No matter where you are or what you're facing, God's love and faithfulness are unwavering. Trust Him to guide you out of the cave and into His marvelous light.

# Chapter 1 – Entering the Cave: David's Story

God anointed David as king in his youth, and he figured it would be a smooth transition to the throne now that he is grown. Boy, was he wrong! One minute Saul was listening to him play the harp, treating him like a son, and the next he tried to kill him! The giant slayer found himself on shaky ground in his heart and hiding in a dark, desolate cave, fearing for his life. Knowing that one step outside could mean death.

The cave was cold and damp, a stark contrast to the warmth of the palace where he had once played his harp for King Saul. The memory of those days seemed distant, almost as if they belonged to another life. David could still hear the soothing melodies in his mind. But now, the same hands that played music to calm Saul's spirit were clenched in fear and frustration.

It all started so well. At first, Saul welcomed him with open arms. David's prowess as a warrior and his musical talent made him a favorite in the court. He had been like a son to Saul, sharing in the king's triumphs and sorrows. But as David's popularity grew, so did

*Saul's jealousy. The people's support of the young shepherd boy had driven a wedge between them.*

*David tried to serve Saul faithfully, but the king's paranoia made him mad. One night, as David played the harp, he saw the flash of a spear out of the corner of his eye. Saul's face twisted with rage as he hurled the weapon at David, narrowly missing him. From that moment on, David knew he had to flee for his life.*

*Huddled in the cave, David prayed, seeking strength and direction. He poured out his heart to God, asking for guidance. As he prayed, a sense of peace began to settle over him. The path ahead was uncertain, and the dangers were real, but David felt a renewed resolve. He was not alone; God was with him, guiding him through the darkness. The anointing of his youth was not a promise of an easy journey but a call to trust in God's plan, even when the way seemed impossible.*

In the depths of the cave, David experienced a profound transformation. His honest prayers and unwavering faith forged a deeper connection with God, preparing him for the challenges ahead. The cave was not the end of David's story but a crucial chapter in his journey to becoming the king God had anointed him to be.

David's experience in the cave teaches us valuable lessons about our own dark seasons. When you find yourself in a metaphorical cave, overwhelmed by life's challenges, remember David's example. Cry out to God with honesty, acknowledging your fears and frustrations. Trust that God is watching over you, even when you feel abandoned. Surround yourself with a supportive community and find strength in shared faith and experiences.

Ultimately, the cave is not a place of defeat but a crucible of faith. It is where your raw, unfiltered prayers meet God's unwavering presence. Just as David emerged from the cave strengthened and prepared for his destiny, you too can find hope and healing in your darkest seasons through honest prayer and steadfast faith.

# True Story

It was a late night in my dorm room, and I was trying to study for an important test. The quiet hours of the night seemed perfect for focusing, but instead of concentrating on my notes, negative thoughts rushed in. Thoughts like "You're not going to make it" and "You will never graduate" popped into my head, and I refused to leave. As they lingered, tears welled up in my eyes because I felt utterly helpless to stop them.

I tried to push through, to force myself to focus on the textbook in front of me, but the weight of those thoughts was too heavy. My heart pounded with anxiety, and the tears that had been gathering finally began to fall. Defeated, I closed my books and decided to go to bed, hoping that sleep would offer an escape from the turmoil in my mind.

But sleep did not come easily. I lay there, tossing and turning, the darkness of the room amplifying the darkness of my thoughts. The despair felt overwhelming, and I didn't know what to do. In my desperation, I reached for the Bible that was sitting on my nightstand. Holding it tightly, I simply cried out into the night, "Jesus! Jesus, help me."

In that moment, something changed. It was as if a profound peace washed over me, a sense of comfort that I had never experienced before. My tears continued to flow, but they were now accompanied by a feeling of release. I felt heard, seen, and held. This was the first time I experienced God's power in helping me at my weakest moment.

Little did I know, this was only the beginning of the story. That night marked a turning point in my faith journey, and I didn't even know it yet.

**Real-Life Application**

1.  Have you been in a deeply hopeless situation?

_______________________________________________

_______________________________________________

_______________________________________________

_______________________________________________

2.  How did you react to it?

_________________________________________________

_________________________________________________

_________________________________________________

_________________________________________________

# Chapter 2 - I Cry Out to the Lord: The Power of Honest Prayer

*I cry aloud to the Lord; I lift up my voice to the Lord for mercy.*
*Psalm 142:1*

David's cry from the cave captures the essence of honest prayer. In his moment of deepest despair, David didn't whisper a polite request or recite a well-crafted prayer. He cried aloud, lifting his voice in a raw, unfiltered plea for God's mercy. This kind of honesty in prayer is both powerful and transformative, offering a model for how you can approach God in your own times of need.

Honest prayer acknowledges your human frailty and your need for divine intervention. It's easy to fall into the trap of thinking you must present yourself as composed and in control, even before God.

For a long time, I felt I needed to look like I had it all figured out, even when my heart was in turmoil. It wasn't until I began to pour out my true feelings—my fears, frustrations, and doubts—that I experienced a profound sense of peace and connection with God.

In the cave, David's cries were not just about seeking relief from his immediate danger. They were also about seeking a deeper connection with God. By lifting his voice and crying aloud, David was reaffirming his trust in God's ability to hear and respond. This act of faith, expressed through honest prayer, reinforced his reliance on God and belief that God cared about his plight.

The power of honest prayer also lies in its ability to transform you. When you lay bare your soul before God, you are often met with a profound sense of peace and clarity. This doesn't mean your circumstances will immediately change, but it does mean that your perspective can shift. You begin to see your struggles in the light of God's presence and promises, which brings a sense of hope and resilience. David's honest prayers in the cave were a turning point, a place where his despair began to transform into trust and his fear into faith.

Moreover, honest prayer builds intimacy with God. Just as in any relationship, openness and transparency are key to deepening the bond. When you approach God with your true self, you move beyond superficial interactions and into a deeper, more meaningful connection. This intimacy with God provides a strong foundation that can sustain you through even the darkest of times.

Remember this: God already knows what is in your heart and on your mind. You might wonder, "Why do I need to say it out loud?" Let's explore the necessity of praying aloud.

Humans are naturally inclined to hide their actions and feelings. Adam and Eve tried to cover their sin with leaves. Joseph's brothers sold him into slavery and convinced their father that he had died. David attempted to conceal a cold-blooded murder on the battlefield. The Pharisees kept their judgments of Jesus's teaching in their hearts. In each instance, the hidden truth was eventually exposed, and I imagine the time between hiding their actions and being exposed was not pleasant. God knows it isn't good for us to bottle things up inside.

What are you bottling up inside? Anger over something that didn't go the way you hoped? Shame because you can't seem to shake the negative thoughts creeping in? Regret over past mistakes? Doubt about whether God hears you at all? Tell Him. Tell God ALL of it.

Being honest in prayer isn't a weekly newsletter to God notifying Him of updates; it's a way of letting go instead of letting the darkness eat you up from the inside out.

In your own life, don't be afraid to cry aloud to the Lord. Bring Him your worries, your fears, your frustrations. Let your prayers be honest and unguarded. Trust that God hears you and that He cares deeply for you. In doing so, you'll discover the transformative power of honest prayer, just as David did. You'll find that, even in your darkest moments, God's mercy and presence are only a heartfelt cry away.

# True Story

The storm inside me had been brewing for weeks, a whirlwind of thoughts and emotions with nowhere to go. Each day, I felt the pressure mounting like a volcano ready to erupt. I was angry, seething with rage, because it felt like God had led me into a bad marriage. The shame others cast upon me for leaving weighed heavily on my heart. I questioned God endlessly, sometimes feeling as though my cries fell on deaf ears.

On the surface, I seemed to be getting back on my feet. I was holding down a job, and to the outside world, it looked like I was healing. But inside, a tempest raged. Then, one day, as I sat alone in silence, the storm broke loose. I could no longer contain the tumultuous thoughts and emotions. In a fit of frustration, I began hurling pillows across the room, tears streaming down my face, and I yelled at God. "Why did you let this happen to me?" "How am I supposed to trust You now?"

Exhausted, I collapsed to my knees, sobbing uncontrollably. Suddenly, a Bible verse echoed in my mind: "Fear not, for I am with you. Do not be dismayed, for I am your God. I will strengthen you. I will help you" (Isaiah 41:10). In that moment, it felt as though a heavy backpack I had been carrying was lifted off my shoulders. A profound peace, one I hadn't felt in what seemed like forever, washed over me.

Honest prayer became the key to unlocking healing in the deepest parts of my soul. It wasn't about having all the answers or an immediate sense of relief. It was about opening up to God, laying bare my burdens, and finding solace in His unwavering presence. As I continued to pour out my heart, I felt His comforting embrace, realizing that He had been there all along, ready to carry my burdens and guide me through the storm.

**Real-Life Application**

1. What is your biggest fear, doubt, or frustration right now?

_______________________________________________

_______________________________________________

_______________________________________________

_______________________________________________

2. Do you believe  God already knows what's in your heart and mind?

_______________________________________________

_______________________________________________

_______________________________________________

_______________________________________________

3. What stops you from being honest in your prayers?

_______________________________________________

_______________________________________________

_______________________________________________

_______________________________________________

# Chapter 3 - Telling My Trouble: Being Vulnerable with God

*I pour out before him my complaint; before him, I tell my trouble.*

*Psalm 142:2*

David's words in Psalm 142:2 highlight the profound act of being vulnerable with God. In this single verse, he shows us the importance of laying our burdens before the Lord. Being vulnerable with God is not about presenting a polished version of our problems but about pouring out our hearts unfiltered. This kind of transparency fosters a deeper, more authentic relationship with God and allows us to experience His comfort and guidance in our darkest times.

In moments of distress, you might feel the urge to bottle up your emotions, fearing that they are too messy or insignificant to bring to God. Yet, David's example teaches that there is no trouble too small or too great to share with the Lord. When you pour out your complaint and tell your trouble, you acknowledge your need for God and invite Him into your struggle. This act of faith affirms that you trust God to handle your deepest pains.

Being vulnerable with God requires courage. It means admitting that you cannot manage everything on your own and that you need His help. This admission is not a sign of weakness but a recognition of your human limitations and God's infinite strength. When you open up to God about your fears, frustrations, and doubts, you allow Him to work in your life in ways that might not be possible if you keep those feelings hidden.

David's approach in Psalm 142 is a model for you. He didn't hold back; he expressed his feelings freely and openly. By doing so, he not only found solace but also strengthened his relationship with God. When you follow David's example and pour out your complaints before the Lord, you open yourself to His healing presence. You invite Him to intervene in your situation and to bring His peace and comfort to your troubled heart.

Telling your troubles to God is a powerful practice that can transform your spiritual life. It helps you to release the burdens that weigh you down and to trust in God's ability to carry them for you. By being vulnerable with God, you experience His compassion and care in a profound way, reminding you that you are never alone in your struggles.

Let's be honest for a minute: complaining is nothing new for us. We often find something to complain about on any given day. Sometimes, it's as simple as traffic moving too slowly on the morning commute or the Internet browser not loading as quickly as it did 10 minutes ago. Other times, it's as challenging as navigating a cancer diagnosis or grieving the loss of a parent. Wherever your complaints fall on the spectrum, God is aware, and He does care. However, He cares more about your heart than simply removing the obstacle.

Being vulnerable to God is essential. Traffic moving slow? Tell God how you feel about it, but don't let it boil into road rage. Lost a parent recently? Tell God how you feel, allow yourself to grieve, and let God heal your sorrow.

Every moment of complaint is an opportunity, and you do have a choice. You can air it out to all your friends or let it consume your heart, OR you can be vulnerable with God, sharing your burdens and allowing Him to carry them for you.

As you journey through life's challenges, remember that God is always ready to listen. He invites you to pour out your heart, to tell Him your troubles, and to lean on Him for support. You will find that His love and grace are more than sufficient to meet your every need, bringing light to your darkest moments.

# True Story

During a particularly busy season of life, I noticed a subtle shift in my routine. My prayer life, once a source of strength, had dwindled. The demands of college life had taken over, and without realizing it, I replaced my conversations with God with venting sessions with my friends.

Looking back over the last few months, I noticed a trend. I wasn't going through anything particularly heartbreaking. It was the usual college chaos: a professor acting weird, a roommate doing something annoying, or my coffee not being hot enough. Yet, I found myself complaining to friends more often than talking to God. The temporary relief from venting to friends was just that – temporary. The weight of my frustrations always returned the next day.

One evening, after a particularly frustrating day, I decided to try something different. Instead of reaching for my phone to call a friend, I sat down in my room and began to pray. I poured out my heart to God, detailing every small annoyance and frustration. It felt strange at first, but as I continued, a sense of peace washed over me.

God was listening, truly listening, and He cared about even the smallest details of my life.

This moment marked the beginning of incorporating complaints into my prayer life. I know it sounds weird, but I encourage you to try it. When I began venting to God, He brought peace and perspective to my situation, helping my heart attitude remain consistent. My challenges didn't disappear, but they no longer seemed as overwhelming. Sharing my burdens with God didn't just bring temporary relief; it brought lasting peace. It transformed my approach to prayer and deepened my relationship with God, proving that even our smallest complaints can be a pathway to His presence and peace.

**Real-Life Application**

1. Who do you tell your problems to first?

______________________________

______________________________

______________________________

______________________________

2. What specific complaint can you take to God today?

___________________________________________________

___________________________________________________

___________________________________________________

___________________________________________________

# Chapter 4 - When My Spirit Grows Faint: Finding Strength in Weakness

*When my spirit grows faint within me... Psalm 142:3a*

There are moments in life when you feel utterly exhausted, both physically and spiritually. Times when the weight of your burdens makes it difficult to even lift your head. In Psalm 142:3a, David captures this sentiment perfectly: "When my spirit grows faint within me..." These words resonate deeply because they echo the universal experience of feeling overwhelmed and powerless. Yet, it is precisely in these moments of weakness that you can find true strength.

David's honesty about his own frailty is a powerful reminder that feeling weak is not a failure; it is a part of being human. When your spirit grows faint, it is a signal that you need to turn to God for strength. Acknowledging your limitations and seeking God's help is not an admission of defeat but an act of faith. It's in recognizing your own insufficiency that you open yourself to God's all-sufficient power.

In my own life, there have been times when I felt completely drained, with no energy or hope left to face the challenges before me – I was depressed. It was in these dark moments I learned the true meaning of relying on God.

It's okay to admit that you don't have it all together. When you are honest with God about your feelings of faintness, you give Him the opportunity to come alongside you and carry you through. God's response to your weakness is not one of disappointment but of compassion and support.

Finding strength in weakness involves shifting your focus from your own limitations to God's limitless power. It's about trusting that He is with you, even when you feel most vulnerable.

When you feel like you can't go on, remember God is your strength. Instead of trying to muster strength from within, lean on God and let Him sustain you. This dependence on God transforms your experience of weakness into an opportunity for His power to be displayed in your life.

What comes to mind when you think of the word "weakness"? In our culture, weakness is often viewed as a sign of failure or something to be exploited. Men are taught that physical strength is admirable while physical weakness is undesirable. Women are encouraged to display emotional strength, while emotional distress is seen as a flaw. Our society tries to define these concepts without considering God's perspective.

However, when Paul writes, "For when I am weak, then I am strong" (2 Corinthians 12:10b), he isn't claiming his own strength. Let's look at the full context of his statement:

"But He (Jesus) said to me, 'My grace is sufficient for you, for my power is made perfect in weakness.' Therefore, I will boast all the more gladly of my weaknesses so that the power of Christ may rest upon me. For the sake of Christ, then, I am content with weaknesses, insults, hardships, persecutions, and calamities. For when I am weak, then I am strong" (2 Corinthians 12:9-10).

Paul boasts of his weaknesses because they reveal God's power. Often, it's not until we reach the end of our own strength and acknowledge our faint spirit that we truly experience the fullness of God's power in our lives.

Don't be afraid to admit when your spirit grows faint. Embrace those moments as invitations to deepen your reliance on God. Let His strength fill your weakness, His hope replace your despair, and His presence be your comfort. In your weakest moments, you will find that God's strength is more than enough to carry you through.

# True Story

After a night of wrestling with vivid nightmares and barely getting any sleep, the sound of my alarm was a cruel reminder of the new day. Physically, I felt too weak to even consider getting out of bed. My eyes were puffy from crying, and emotionally, I was utterly drained. Spiritually, I felt exhausted and disconnected.

As I lay there, I told God I didn't want to go to work today. I didn't even want to stand up. The comfort of my bed seemed like the only safe place in the world. But as I continued to pray, a flicker of courage began to grow within me. Slowly, I felt the resolve to face the day, even though I didn't feel ready in any way.

I forced myself to put on some clothes, ate a quick breakfast, and got into my car. Driving to the office, every part of me wanted to turn around and go back home. When I arrived, my eyes were still puffy, and I was walking slower than usual. My brain felt foggy, and I knew I wasn't operating at my best.

Despite everything, I sat down at my desk and began working. Each task felt like an uphill battle, but somehow, God gave me the strength to push through. Hours passed, and bit by bit, I completed my work. By the end of the day, I had successfully finished a project that I had been dreading.

Looking back, I realized that God had carried me through the day. He provided the strength I lacked and helped me accomplish what seemed impossible. Even in my weakest moments, He was there, guiding me and giving me the courage to keep going.

## Real-Life Application

1. Do you believe weakness is a sign of failure? Why?

_______________________________________________

_______________________________________________

_______________________________________________

_______________________________________________

2. How can you depend on God today?

_______________________________________________

_______________________________________________

_______________________________________________

_______________________________________________

# Chapter 5 - You Know My Way: Trusting in God's Guidance

*...it is you who watch over my way. Psalm 142:3b*

In the midst of uncertainty and chaos, finding your way can feel impossible. When David declared, "It is you who watch over my way," he affirmed a profound truth: God is intimately aware of your journey and steps. Trusting in God's guidance is essential, especially when the path ahead is unclear and you feel lost.

David's life was marked by many instances where he had to rely on God's direction. From fleeing King Saul to leading a nation, David experienced firsthand the necessity of trusting God's guidance. His words in Psalm 142:3b reflect a deep-seated confidence that God was always watching over him, even in the most perilous times. This same confidence can be yours.

Trusting in God's guidance begins with acknowledging that He knows your way better than you do. He sees the entire path laid out before you, from beginning to end, and understands every twist and turn. When you trust Him, you are choosing to rely on His omniscience rather than your limited perspective. This trust is not blind but is based on the knowledge that God's ways are higher and His plans are perfect.

In my own life, there have been countless times when I've had to trust God's guidance despite not seeing the full picture. One particular instance stands out: I was facing a major decision, and the options before me seemed equally daunting. I felt overwhelmed and unsure of which direction to take. In my prayers, I poured out my confusion and fears to God. Gradually, through scripture, the counsel of trusted friends, and a deep sense of peace that surpassed understanding, I discerned God's guidance. Looking back, I can see how His hand was directing my steps all along.

David's assertion that God watches over our way assures us that we are never alone in our journey. God is actively involved in our lives, orchestrating circumstances, opening doors, and providing direction. When you trust in His guidance, you are placing your life in the hands of the One who knows every detail and loves you infinitely.

To cultivate trust in God's guidance, begin by seeking Him through prayer and scripture. Prayer is your direct line of communication with God, where you can share your concerns and seek His direction. Scripture provides the foundation of His promises and principles, offering clarity and wisdom. As you immerse yourself in God's word, you'll find His guidance becomes more evident through the power of the Holy Spirit.

Additionally, surround yourself with a community of believers who can offer support and discernment. God often uses others to speak into our lives and provide the guidance we need. Their experiences and insights can illuminate your path and reinforce your trust in God's leading.

Finally, remember that trusting in God's guidance doesn't mean the absence of difficulties or detours. It means having confidence that God is with you through it all, working everything for your good. When the path seems unclear, and you feel lost, hold onto the promise that God watches over your way. His guidance is sure, His presence is constant, and His love is unwavering.

# True Story

The decision loomed over me like a dark cloud, and I wrestled with it for days. Moving away from everything I had ever known felt like leaping off a cliff into the unknown. Yet, deep down, I sensed that this was exactly what God wanted me to do.

After earning my degree, uncertainty about the next step weighed heavily on my mind. I constantly sought God's guidance while scouring for opportunities. One day, I stumbled upon an internship program offering to pay for a master's degree, but with a catch: I had to be willing to move anywhere in North America.

Excited yet apprehensive, I began filling out applications for various places. With each submission, I prayed, asking God to open the right door and close all the others. Doors started closing one by one until a single door remained open, nearly 1,000 miles away from my small hometown in Louisiana. The destination? Cincinnati, Ohio.

The idea of leaving my family and friends behind felt daunting. Still, I proceeded with a phone interview and then visited in person, praying for wisdom, clarity, and understanding at every step.

One day, while on my knees, reading the Bible, and pouring out my heart to God, I heard a gentle whisper, "Go make disciples." It was at that moment I knew what I had to do. Trusting His guidance, I made the bold decision to move.

Leaving my small town for Cincinnati was a leap of faith. It wasn't easy, but it taught me to stop and listen to God's guidance and to be willing to go when He says go. The journey was transformative, deepening my trust in God and His plans for my life and showing me that sometimes the hardest decisions lead to the most rewarding paths.

**Real-Life Application**

1. How often do you seek God's guidance when making decisions?

____________________________________________

____________________________________________

____________________________________________

____________________________________________

2.  What community of believers do you surround yourself
    with?

    ___________________________________________________

    ___________________________________________________

    ___________________________________________________

    ___________________________________________________

# Chapter 6 - Hidden Traps: Recognizing and Avoiding Spiritual Pitfalls

*In the path where I walk, people have hidden a snare for me.*

*Psalm 142:3c*

David's words paint a vivid picture of the dangers lurking along the journey of faith. He speaks of snares hidden in his path, emphasizing the reality of spiritual pitfalls that can entangle and derail us. Recognizing and avoiding these spiritual pitfalls is crucial for maintaining a strong and steadfast walk with God, especially when you are struggling with depression.

Depression itself can be a spiritual pitfall, but within it, there are specific traps that can further complicate your journey. These pitfalls can be particularly subtle and insidious, preying on your vulnerability during your darkest seasons.

One of the most common spiritual pitfalls during depression is the temptation to isolate yourself. Depression often brings feelings of shame and unworthiness, making you want to withdraw from others. This isolation can lead to a sense of disconnection from God and your faith community. David, too, felt isolated in his cave, hiding from his enemies. To avoid this trap, it's essential to reach out for support, even when it feels difficult. Stay connected with trusted friends, family, or a counselor who can offer encouragement and remind you of God's love and presence.

Another hidden trap is the distortion of your self-worth. Depression can whisper lies that you are unworthy, unloved, or beyond redemption. These lies can be deeply convincing and lead to a spiral of negative self-talk and hopelessness. To combat this, immerse yourself in God's truth. Regularly read and meditate on scriptures that affirm your identity in Christ. Remember you are fearfully and wonderfully made, loved unconditionally by God, and that His grace is sufficient for you, no matter how you feel.

A particularly dangerous pitfall during depression is the temptation to numb your pain with unhealthy behaviors. This can include substance abuse, excessive screen time, or other forms of escapism. These temporary fixes can further distance you from God and exacerbate your depression. Instead, seek healthy coping mechanisms that draw you closer to God. Engage in activities that uplift your spirit, such as prayer, worship, and reading the Psalms, which resonate deeply during times of distress.

Depression can also make you susceptible to doubting God's goodness and presence. When you are in the depths of despair, it can feel like God is distant or indifferent to your suffering. This doubt can erode your faith and lead to spiritual apathy. David's honesty in Psalm 142 shows that it's okay to express your doubts and fears to God. Pour out your heart to Him, telling Him about your struggles and seeking His comfort. Trust that God hears your cries and is with you, even when His presence feels elusive.

In my own journey, I have encountered various spiritual pitfalls while struggling with depression. One notable experience involved a season where I felt completely disconnected from God and my community. I isolated myself, believing that no one could understand my pain. It wasn't until I reached out for help and allowed others into my struggle that I began to see glimpses of God's light and love through their support.

David's acknowledgment of hidden snares in his path reminds you that vigilance and reliance on God are essential. He trusted in God's guidance to navigate these dangers, and you can do the same. Pray for discernment to recognize potential pitfalls and for strength to resist them. Surround yourself with a supportive faith community that encourages you and holds you accountable.

Recognizing and avoiding spiritual pitfalls requires a proactive approach. Stay rooted in God's Word, prioritize your relationship with Him, and seek the wisdom of fellow believers. As you do, you'll be better equipped to identify the snares along your path and navigate them with confidence.

By staying vigilant and trusting in His guidance, you can avoid the hidden traps and continue to walk faithfully in His light, even in the midst of depression.

# True Story

The transition to life after my divorce felt like being a frog slowly simmering in a pot of boiling water. At first, the changes seemed subtle, almost imperceptible. The COVID-19 pandemic had transformed daily life into a strange new reality, and I found myself navigating the aftermath of my personal upheaval amidst social distancing and a bizarre work schedule.

Working from home was a double-edged sword. Without the routine of commuting, I began to slip into bad habits. Mornings blurred into afternoons, and I found myself staying up later than ever before. The absence of a structured schedule meant that I would often eat out of boredom—first just a few grapes, then an extra lunch, and soon an entire chocolate bar after dinner. What started as small indulgences rapidly escalated.

Before I knew it, I was devouring half a gallon of ice cream in two days and waking up at 2 a.m. craving Zebra Cakes and Reese's Peanut Butter Cups. At first, I shrugged it off, dismissing it as a harmless comfort. But the overeating became a desperate escape, a way to numb the heartache that I wasn't ready to face.

I was trapped in a vicious cycle: using food to soothe my emotional pain while spiraling deeper into shame. It became a way to escape from the loneliness and the turmoil of a life that felt out of control. The real issue, however, was that I was avoiding the one thing that could offer true solace—my relationship with God.

In the midst of this unhealthy pattern, I came to a startling realization. The overeating was a symptom of a deeper problem: a disconnect from my spiritual life. I was relying on food as a substitute for God's fellowship, attempting to fill a void that only He could truly address.

Since then, I've taken conscious steps to rectify this. I now watch over this hidden snare carefully, recognizing it for what it is. While I still enjoy chocolate and ice cream, I do so in moderation, ensuring that these treats do not overshadow my commitment to a balanced, healthy lifestyle. I've established a regular routine that includes proper sleep, balanced meals, and, most importantly, a steady prayer life.

My journey has taught me that when I face emotional struggles, it's vital to turn to God rather than seek comfort in fleeting indulgences. Food, once a crutch, has been replaced by a renewed focus on spiritual nourishment. Each day, I ask God to help me avoid the pitfalls I once fell into and to keep my heart and mind aligned with His purpose. This awareness has turned my struggle into a testimony of God's ability to guide us through even the most difficult seasons.

## Real-Life Application

1.  What is a potential trap for you in the cave?

    _______________________________________________

    _______________________________________________

    _______________________________________________

    _______________________________________________

2.  Make a list of 3 proactive steps you can take to avoid these hidden traps.

    _______________________________________________

    _______________________________________________

    _______________________________________________

    _______________________________________________

# Chapter 7 - No One Cares for My Life: Overcoming Feelings of Abandonment

*Look and see, there is no one at my right hand; no one is concerned for me. I have no refuge; no one cares for my life.*

*Psalm 142:4*

David's lament in Psalm 142:4 is a poignant expression of deep loneliness and abandonment. His words capture the heart-wrenching feeling that no one cares or understands. This sense of abandonment is a common and devastating experience, especially during times of depression and despair.

Depression often brings with it an overwhelming sense of abandonment. The feelings of isolation and disconnection can make it seem like no one truly cares about your pain. This emotional state can create a mental fog, obscuring the support and love that actually exist around you. David's cry reflects this profound sense of isolation, yet it also opens the door to seeking God's comfort.

When depression takes hold, it's crucial to remember that God is always present, even when it seems like no one else is. He sees your struggles, hears your cries, and is intimately aware of your pain. David's candid expression of his loneliness serves as an invitation to bring your feelings to God. Just as David did, pour out your heart to Him, honestly expressing your hurt and confusion. God is not distant or indifferent; He is a loving Father who cares deeply for you.

In my own journey, I've encountered moments where depression made me feel utterly abandoned. There was a time when I faced a significant personal crisis, and I believed no one understood or cared about what I was going through. Despite the support around me, the weight of my feelings isolated me. In those dark moments, I turned to God, shared my deepest pain, and sought His presence. It was through these honest conversations with God that I began to feel His comforting presence and a renewed sense of hope.

David's experience teaches that while human support can falter, God's care never does. When you feel like no one cares for your life, remind yourself of God's promises. Scriptures like Isaiah 41:10, "Fear not, for I am with you; be not dismayed, for I am your God; I will strengthen you, I will help you, I will uphold you with my righteous right hand," affirm that God is with you, providing strength and support.

To overcome feelings of abandonment, actively seek out God's presence. Engage in practices that draw you closer to Him, such as prayer, worship, and reading the Bible. Surround yourself with a community of believers who can offer support and remind you of God's love. Even when you feel isolated, remember that you are part of the body of Christ, a community designed to support and uplift one another.

Another practical step is to serve others. Reaching out to those in need can shift your focus from your own pain to the needs of others, creating a sense of connection and purpose.

David's lament also serves as a reminder to be mindful of those around you who might be feeling abandoned. Your empathy and support can make a significant difference in someone else's life. By offering a listening ear, a kind word, or practical help, you can reflect God's love and care to those in need.

In conclusion, while feelings of abandonment can be overwhelming, they are not insurmountable. By turning to God and embracing His presence, you can overcome these feelings and find refuge in His unwavering love. Remember, even when it seems like no one cares, God is always there, watching over you and holding you close. His love is constant, His care is profound, and His presence is a refuge you can always rely on.

# True Story

In the bustling world of early college life, I often found myself caught between the rush of meeting new people and the quiet solitude of my dorm room. The campus was teeming with faces, yet the social whirl seemed only to deepen my sense of isolation. I struggled with the question, "Does anyone actually care about me?" Despite the constant influx of acquaintances, I spent many evenings alone, studying in the dim light of my room, the weight of loneliness pressing heavily on my shoulders.

My introverted nature made it all too easy to retreat into my shell, convinced that my so-called friends were merely passing shadows in the whirlwind of campus life. It was simpler to shut myself away rather than reach out as my mind spun stories of neglect and indifference. In my heart, I grappled with a growing belief that if they didn't care about me, then why should I bother caring about them?

Then, one day, as I returned to my dorm room after a particularly grueling set of classes, something unusual caught my eye. Perched on my bookshelf was a small aquarium, a delicate bubble of serenity amidst the clutter of textbooks and papers. Inside, a single fish swam gracefully, its gentle movements a stark contrast to my restless thoughts. Attached to the aquarium was a note, its cheerful scrawl an unexpected warmth against my chill of isolation.

The note revealed that a couple of my classmates had come together to gift me this small creature. Their intention was simple yet profound: to provide me with a bit of companionship in my dorm room, a reminder that I was not alone while I studied or read. This gesture, though modest, was a beacon of light in my dimly lit room and a balm to my bruised heart.

Here was tangible proof that, despite my self-imposed isolation and the swirling doubts in my mind, there were people who cared and who were willing to step out and make a difference in my life. It was a reminder that God had not left me in my loneliness but had provided a community around me, often hidden behind the veil of my own perspective.

It became a lesson in recognizing the subtle signs of God's provision. Sometimes, our own thoughts and fears can obscure the support and love that are always present, waiting for us to see beyond our self-imposed barriers. This small aquarium was more than just a decorative piece; it was a reminder to trust that even in times of doubt, God surrounds us with care and community, often disguised as the everyday gestures of those who walk alongside us.

# Real-Life Application

1.  Are feelings of abandonment consuming you?

    ______________________________________________

    ______________________________________________

    ______________________________________________

    ______________________________________________

2.  Tell God your first step toward trusting He is always
    with you.

    ______________________________________________

    ______________________________________________

    ______________________________________________

    ______________________________________________

# Chapter 8 - You Are My Refuge: Finding Safety in God's Presence

*I cry to you, Lord; I say, "You are my refuge, my portion in the land of the living." Psalm 142:5*

David's declaration in Psalm 142:5 reveals a profound truth about God's character and His role in our lives. In moments of intense struggle and fear, David turns to God, acknowledging Him as his refuge and portion. This verse is a testament to the safety and security found in God's presence, especially when life's circumstances feel overwhelming and despair looms large.

When you face your own dark seasons, feelings of vulnerability and insecurity can be all-consuming. Depression, anxiety, and life's pressures can create a sense of being trapped, much like David in his cave. In these moments, it's essential to follow David's example and turn to God, recognizing Him as your refuge. God's presence offers a sanctuary, a place where you can find peace and safety even in the midst of chaos.

Finding safety in God's presence involves actively seeking Him and resting in His promises. One practical way to do this is through prayer. Prayer is a powerful tool that connects you directly with God, allowing you to pour out your heart and receive His comfort.

Another way to find refuge in God is by immersing yourself in His Word. The Bible is filled with promises and reminders of God's faithfulness. Verses like Psalm 46:1, "God is our refuge and strength, an ever-present help in trouble," provide assurance that God is always with you, ready to offer His protection and support. Meditating on these scriptures can strengthen your faith and reinforce the truth that God is your safe haven.

Worship also plays a crucial role in experiencing God's presence. When you worship, you shift your focus from your problems to God's greatness. Worship is not just about singing songs; it's about declaring God's goodness and sovereignty over your life. In worship, you can experience a tangible sense of God's presence, which brings peace and comfort. David, a skilled musician and worshipper, often turned to music to express his reliance on God, and you can do the same.

Safety can mean different things to different people. For some, it's about having every door equipped with deadbolts and security cameras. For others, it's as simple as locking all the doors before bed. While these examples pertain to physical safety, feeling secure in God's presence goes beyond the tangible.

Think about times when you've felt uneasy around someone without knowing why or when you've hesitated to open up. These feelings are often subtle cues from God, guiding us away from people or situations that might not be safe. True safety in a relationship means you can be yourself—without pretense or fear of judgment. It's the freedom to express your emotions, be silly, and share your thoughts openly, knowing you'll be accepted.

In the quiet of your prayers, does a sense of safety embrace you? Do you trust that God's presence wraps around you like a warm blanket, offering comfort and reassurance? Even when the world feels uncertain, remember that with God, you are always in a place where you can be truly vulnerable, free from the fear of rejection or harm.

It's important to remember that finding safety in God's presence doesn't mean you will be free from difficulties. David still faced numerous challenges, but his faith in God provided him with the strength to endure. Similarly, your trust in God as your refuge will give you the resilience to navigate life's hardships. God's presence doesn't eliminate your problems, but it changes your perspective and equips you to face them with hope and confidence.

No matter what you face, you can find safety in His presence. Trust in Him, seek Him earnestly, and rest in the assurance that He is your refuge. In His presence, you will find the peace and strength to endure, knowing that He is always with you, providing shelter and comfort in every storm.

# True Story

In my friendships, I've discovered that true safety often comes in the form of silent companionship—a rare but cherished gift. When I'm with friends, and we can sit together in complete silence, without the need for conversation, I feel utterly secure. But recently, the busyness of work, life, and family had begun to crowd my space, and I longed for a retreat from it all.

I decided on a spontaneous road trip to Sedona, Arizona, a place that was unfamiliar but intriguing. I booked a quaint bed and breakfast, eager for a change of scenery. The days were filled with delightful local eateries and charming sights, but it was the early mornings that I looked forward to the most.

Each dawn, while the air was still cool enough to wear a hoodie, I would rise before the sun and head out among the red rocks. There, nestled in the serenity of nature, I found my solace. I would sit quietly, my Bible open but mostly untouched, allowing the peace of the surroundings to wash over me. The silence was profound, and it became my sanctuary.

In those moments, I didn't need to seek out a divine revelation or expect a dramatic spiritual experience. Instead, I found that the gentle presence of God was all I needed. Without the distractions of daily life—no phone, no email notifications, just the pure, unspoiled beauty of creation—I could simply be. The rustling of the breeze, the warmth of the sunrise, and the majestic stillness of the rocks spoke volumes, reassuring me that God's presence was enough.

**Real-Life Application**

1. How long has it been since you've soaked in God's presence, either through worship music, scripture reading, or silence?

_______________________________________________

_______________________________________________

_______________________________________________

_______________________________________________

2.  I encourage you to put this book down and spend 10

minutes in God's presence today.

_______________________________________________

_______________________________________________

_______________________________________________

_______________________________________________

# Chapter 9 - I Am in Desperate Need: Admitting Our Dependence on God

*Listen to my cry, for I am in desperate need; rescue me from those who pursue me, for they are too strong for me. Psalm 142:6*

David's plea reflects a moment of profound vulnerability and dependence on God. He acknowledges his desperate need for rescue, recognizing that his enemies are too strong for him to overcome on his own. This verse encapsulates the essence of admitting our dependence on God, especially in times of overwhelming adversity and distress.

Throughout his life, David faced numerous challenges and enemies who sought to harm him. From the lion and the bear he confronted as a shepherd boy to the formidable Goliath on the battlefield and even King Saul's relentless pursuit, David's journey was marked by constant threats and dangers. Despite his courage and military prowess, David knew that some adversaries were beyond his strength to defeat. In Psalm 142, he turns to God, acknowledging his inability to overcome these powerful foes without divine intervention.

When you find yourself in desperate circumstances, whether facing external threats or battling internal struggles like depression or anxiety, admitting your dependence on God is a crucial step toward finding strength and deliverance. It requires humility to acknowledge that your own efforts are insufficient and that you need God.

In my own life, there have been moments when I felt overwhelmed by challenges that seemed insurmountable. During these times, I had to confront my pride and self-sufficiency, recognizing that I couldn't handle everything on my own. Admitting my dependence on God was not a sign of weakness but a recognition of His sovereignty and power.

Admitting our dependence on God also involves surrendering control. It's a recognition that God's ways are higher than our ways, and His plans are often beyond our understanding. This surrender requires trust and faith that God is working all things together for your good, even when circumstances seem dire.

Finding the courage to admit your dependence on God may also involve seeking support from others. Surround yourself with a community of believers who can pray for you, offer encouragement, and stand with you during difficult times. Together, you can strengthen one another's faith and witness the power of God's intervention in your lives.

As you navigate your own challenges and struggles, remember that admitting your dependence on God is a declaration of faith. It is an acknowledgment that God is your refuge and strength, ready to rescue you from every adversary and circumstance that threatens to overwhelm you. Embrace your dependence on God, knowing that He is faithful to hear your cries, respond to your needs, and deliver you according to His perfect will.

# True Story

From a young age, I wore my independence like a badge of honor. As a middle schooler, I was already waking up to my alarm, handling laundry, and holding a key to our house so I could let myself in after school. My mom's trust in me only fueled my desire to prove I could manage everything on my own.

One afternoon, that fierce independence was put to the test. I came home from school and realized, to my horror, that I had locked my key inside the house. The logical thing to do would have been to walk down the road to city hall and borrow a phone. But my pride had other plans. Determined to solve the problem myself, I found an open window and stacked a wobbly tower of buckets beneath it. With a mixture of determination and stubbornness, I clambered up and hurled myself inside. In my haste, I forgot to lift my legs, leaving painful bruises down my shins. For days, my legs ached, but I took it as a price for maintaining my independence.

This tendency didn't fade as I grew older. As an adult, I still try to carry all my groceries in one trip, arms straining under the weight. When something breaks, I stubbornly try to fix it myself before even considering asking for help. Each time, God gently reminds me that He didn't design us to bear burdens alone but to lean on Him.

I realize that true strength lies not in solitary independence but in the humble admission of our need for God. Each bruise and struggle serves as a reminder that we are not meant to navigate life alone. God's design is for us to lean on Him and find strength in His presence.

Now, I see my journey not as a testament to my independence but as a testament to God's unending patience and love. I've learned to ask for help, to lean on the community around me, and, most importantly, to rely on God. Each day, I'm reminded that my worth isn't measured by my ability to do everything on my own but by my willingness to admit my need for God and His grace.

**Real-Life Application**

1. What comes to mind when you hear the word "dependence"?

_______________________________________________

_______________________________________________

_______________________________________________

_______________________________________________

2. How can you learn to become more dependent on God?

______________________________________________________

______________________________________________________

______________________________________________________

______________________________________________________

# Chapter 10 - Set Me Free from My Prison: Finding Liberation in Christ

*Set me free from my prison... Psalm 142:7a*

The final verse of Psalm 142 starts with a powerful appeal for liberation. Although his literal imprisonment was a cave where he hid from his enemies, this verse speaks to the metaphorical prisons we all encounter—those internal and external struggles that confine us and hinder our freedom.

When you face your own "prisons"—whether they are emotional, spiritual, or circumstantial—the feeling of being trapped can be overwhelming. Depression can be one of the most confining prisons, with walls that seem insurmountable and darkness that feels impenetrable. These prisons isolate you, distort your perception of reality, and drain your hope. Yet, David's cry offers a path to freedom: turning to God and seeking His deliverance.

Finding freedom in Christ begins with acknowledging the prison you are in. Whether it's a struggle with sin, mental health issues, or life's overwhelming challenges, the first step is to bring these issues into the light of God's presence. David's openness about his problem models the honesty and vulnerability required to seek true freedom. When you admit your struggles and cry out to God, you open the door for His healing and liberation.

Immersing yourself in the truths of God's Word is another step on the road to freedom. Scriptures such as John 8:36, "So if the Son sets you free, you will be free indeed," reinforce the promise of freedom in Christ. Meditate on these truths, allowing them to penetrate your heart and mind. Let them replace the lies and fears that keep you bound.

Christ's mission was to set captives free. In Luke 4:18, Jesus declares, "The Spirit of the Lord is on me… He has sent me to proclaim freedom for the prisoners and recovery of sight for the blind, to set the oppressed free." This proclamation is a powerful reminder that Jesus came to break the chains that bind us. Through His life, death, and resurrection, Jesus offers a freedom that transcends any earthly confinement.

In my own life, I have experienced seasons where I felt imprisoned by my circumstances and emotions. There were times when the weight of depression felt like chains around my heart and mind, preventing me from living fully and freely. During these times, I turned to Christ, seeking His presence and power to break these chains. Through prayer, scripture, and the support of my church community, I began to experience the liberating power of Christ. He met me in my darkest places, offering hope and freedom that I couldn't find on my own.

David's cry, "Set me free from my prison," is a timeless reminder of the freedom available in Christ. No matter what binds you, Jesus offers a way out. Turn to Him, seek His presence, and embrace the freedom He provides. In Christ, you can find true liberation, experiencing a life of joy, peace, and purpose.

# True Story

Since my last name is Free, I often joke that I've been free my whole life! But the truth is, my walk with God has been a journey of Him setting me free from various entanglements. One of the most profound areas where I experienced this freedom was in forgiving my dad.

As a child, I held a grudge against my dad for leaving my mom. This grudge festered, turning me into an angry teenager and eventually a bitter adult. I carried this bitterness with me everywhere, like a heavy cloud that overshadowed my every step. I tried to ignore it, bury it, and even convince myself that forgiveness wasn't necessary. But the more I resisted, the worse things got.

It became a constant burden, a dark cloud that hung over me, affecting my relationships and my outlook on life. The weight of it all became too much to bear. One day, in a moment of desperation, I cried out to God, "Okay, I'm willing to consider letting go." It was the first step toward freedom, but it was far from easy.

The path to forgiveness was long and filled with moments of failure. I had to confront my pain, acknowledge my feelings, and continuously choose to let go of the anger and resentment. There were days when the bitterness threatened to return, but each time, I brought it to God in prayer. Gradually, I felt the weight lifting.

Over time, I began to experience true freedom. The cloud that had loomed over me for so long started to dissipate. The anger and bitterness no longer controlled my life. I found peace in letting go and allowing God to heal the wounds of my past.

Today, I can honestly say I've forgiven my dad. The cloud of unforgiveness no longer lingers in my life. I've learned that true freedom comes not from holding on to grudges but from releasing them to God. My journey of forgiveness has been proof of His power to set us free from the chains that bind us.

### Real-Life Application

1. What is one way your circumstances keep you imprisoned?

____________________________________________________

____________________________________________________

____________________________________________________

____________________________________________________

2. Do you believe Jesus offers freedom for you?

_______________________________________________

_______________________________________________

_______________________________________________

_______________________________________________

# Chapter 11 - That I May Praise Your Name: The Importance of Worship

*...that I may praise your name... Psalm 142:7b*

As David continues, his prayer has a declaration of purpose wrapped in it: "that I may praise your name." This phrase encapsulates a heart of worship and underscores the significance of worship, especially in times of hardship. Worship is not merely a response to God's deliverance but a vital practice that transforms your perspective brings you closer to God, and anchors you in His presence.

David's life was filled with moments of worship, both in times of triumph and despair. His psalms are a testament to the role worship played in his relationship with God. Even while hiding in a cave, fearing for his life, David's desire to praise God did not wane. This longing to worship amidst adversity teaches a profound lesson about the importance of worship in every season of life.

Worship is crucial because it shifts your focus from your circumstances to God's greatness. When you are trapped in a metaphorical cave—be it depression, anxiety, or any life challenge—your vision can become clouded by despair. It reorients your heart and mind towards God, providing clarity and hope.

When you worship, you invite God's presence into your situation. The act of praising God, even when you don't feel like it, can break the chains of negativity and despair. In my own life, there have been times when worship felt like the last thing I wanted to do. Yet, when I chose to praise God despite my feelings, I experienced a profound shift. God's presence became tangible, lifting my spirit and renewing my strength.

Worship also fosters a deeper intimacy with God. It is a means of drawing near to Him, expressing your love, gratitude, and dependence. As you worship, you open your heart to God, allowing Him to speak to you, comfort you, and guide you. This intimate connection is vital for spiritual growth and resilience.

To cultivate a lifestyle of worship, integrate it into your daily routine. Set aside time each day to praise God through prayer, singing, or meditating on His attributes. Use music, nature, or other forms of creative expression to connect with God. Surround yourself with a community that values worship and encourages you to praise God regularly.

Incorporating scripture into your worship is also powerful. The Bible is filled with verses that exalt God's name and declare His greatness. Use these scriptures in your prayers and songs, allowing them to shape your worship and deepen your understanding of God's character.

Lastly, approach worship with a heart of gratitude. Even in the darkest times, there are reasons to thank God. Reflect on His past faithfulness, the blessings you have received, and the promises in His Word. Gratitude fuels worship and helps you maintain a positive outlook, even when life is challenging.

David's declaration, "that I may praise your name," is a reminder of the centrality of worship in the life of a believer. Worship is not just a response to God's deliverance but a vital practice that sustains you through every season. It transforms your perspective, deepens your relationship with God, and serves as a powerful witness to others. Embrace worship as a daily discipline, and you will find that, like David, your heart will be continually drawn to praise God's name, no matter what circumstances you face.

# True Story

One quiet evening in my apartment, the idea of worshipping alone with God sparked my curiosity. Having grown up with the understanding that worship was something you did in church, surrounded by a congregation, the thought of doing it solo felt foreign and, to be honest, a bit daunting. But the desire to connect with God on a deeper level nudged me forward.

I started by trying to replicate the church experience. I played a worship song on my laptop, sang along, and even tried to mimic the collective prayers and reflections. But it all felt forced, almost like I was putting on a one-person show for an audience of one. The awkwardness was palpable, and I knew this wasn't what genuine worship was supposed to feel like.

Determined to find a more authentic way, I began experimenting with different forms of worship. I picked up my guitar and started to sing. At first, my voice wavered, but gradually, the familiar chords and heartfelt lyrics began to feel right. I closed my eyes and let the music flow, not worrying about how I sounded but focusing on who I was singing to.

Next, I opened my Bible and started reading Scripture over various aspects of my life. I paused frequently, letting the words sink in and reflecting on God's character—His goodness, His mercy, His unfailing love. The Scriptures began to resonate deeply, transforming my thoughts and lifting my spirit.

As days turned into weeks, these moments of worship became integral to my daily routine. I discovered that true worship wasn't confined to songs or specific rituals. It was about the heart—expressing love, gratitude, and reverence for God in everything I did. Whether I was singing, praying, serving others, or simply being still in His presence, I found ways to honor Him.

One morning, as the sun cast a golden glow through my window, I realized how much my perspective had shifted. Worship transcended the boundaries of time and place, transforming ordinary moments into opportunities to glorify God. Preparing breakfast became an act of gratitude, each meal a reminder of His provision. Even mundane tasks like washing dishes turned into moments of reflection as I thanked God for the simple blessings of life.

In these everyday acts, I found a profound sense of connection with God. It wasn't about perfecting a performance but about cultivating a genuine relationship. Worship flowed naturally from my heart, a continuous expression of love and devotion. Through this journey, I discovered that worship is less about the method and more about the intention—it's about being present with God, recognizing His presence in every aspect of life, and allowing His love to permeate all that we do.

And so, in the solitude of my apartment, I learned that true worship is about surrender. It's about giving God my whole being, not just in moments of song and prayer but in every breath, every thought, and every action. It's about living a life that continually honors Him, finding joy and purpose in the simple act of being with Him.

**Real-Life Application**

1. What does worship mean to you?

_______________________________________________

_______________________________________________

_______________________________________________

_______________________________________________

2. Commit to incorporating one of the suggestions of this chapter into your personal worship.

_______________________________________

_______________________________________

_______________________________________

_______________________________________

# Chapter 12 - The Righteous Will Gather: Community and Support in Faith

*...the righteous will gather about me...Psalm 142:7c*

As David is wrapping up this prayer, he speaks of the righteous gathering around him. This imagery of community and support is powerful, especially in times of distress. David, a man who knew isolation and fear, found solace in the presence of fellow believers. This chapter explores the vital role of community and support in your faith journey, especially when the darkness closes in.

David's life was a testament to the necessity of supportive relationships. Despite his immense faith and strength, he often relied on others for encouragement and assistance. They gathered around him, providing physical, emotional, and spiritual support.

As a believer, you are not meant to walk through life alone. Community is an essential aspect of Christian life. The Bible emphasizes the importance of fellowship and mutual support among believers. Hebrews 10:24-25 urges, "And let us consider how we may spur one another on toward love and good deeds, not giving up meeting together, as some are in the habit of doing, but encouraging one another—and all the more as you see the Day approaching."

When you face personal "caves," having a supportive community can make a significant difference. Isolation can exacerbate feelings of despair and hopelessness, but the community provides a network of care, prayer, and encouragement. The righteous, those who seek God and live according to His ways, are a source of strength and support.

In my own life, there have been times when the burden of my struggles felt too heavy to bear alone. Friends prayed for me, mentors offered wisdom, and fellow believers simply listened, and God used them to make a profound impact.

Building and nurturing a supportive Christian community involves intentionality. Here are some practical steps to foster your own community:

**Join a Local Church:** Being part of a local church connects you with a broader body of believers who can provide support and encouragement. Participate in worship services, join small groups, and engage in church activities to build relationships.

**Participate in Small Groups:** Small groups or Bible studies offer a more intimate setting for sharing your life and faith. These groups provide a space for honest conversations, prayer, and mutual support.

**Seek Accountability Partners:** Having one or two trusted individuals with whom you can share your struggles and victories provides accountability and encouragement. These relationships are built on trust and mutual respect, helping you stay grounded in your faith.

**Serve Together:** Engaging in service projects or ministry activities with others fosters a sense of unity and purpose. Serving together strengthens bonds and reminds you of the broader mission of the Church.

**Be Vulnerable:** Authentic relationships require vulnerability. Share your struggles and allow others to support you. In turn, be available to listen and support others in their times of need.

**Pray for One Another:** Prayer is a powerful tool for supporting each other. Regularly praying for your community members strengthens your bonds and invites God's presence into your relationships.

In the darkest of times, the presence of fellow believers can be a beacon of hope. Their prayers, words of encouragement, and acts of kindness are tangible expressions of God's love and care. They remind you that you are not alone and that God is with you, working through His people to provide comfort and strength.

As you navigate your own relationship with Christ, remember the importance of community. Seek out and invest in relationships with other believers. Allow the righteous to gather around you, providing the support and encouragement you need. In turn, be a source of support for others, demonstrating the love of Christ through your actions. Together, as a community of faith, you can face the challenges of life with resilience and hope, knowing that God is with you every step of the way.

# True Story

If you're not seeking out community, sometimes it finds you! At least, that was true for me as a college freshman. I was always introverted, with an added dose of social awkwardness when meeting new people. Despite my tendencies, I made an effort to attend the usual freshman events—from burgers in the quad to the late-night pancake breakfast. It was at one of these gatherings that I met a particularly bubbly people person who, to my surprise, invited me to go to church with her.

Looking for a church to be part of, I decided to take her up on the offer. One church invitation turned into exchanging phone numbers, which led to late-night chats, and eventually, she invited me to all sorts of places she went. Before I knew it, I was her late-night companion while she cleaned the church and the introvert she dragged to a Super Bowl party at a friend's house.

She had a knack for inviting me out when I was at my worst. Even when I was annoyed, I still went because it was better than pouting alone in my dorm room. Somehow, she always knew when I needed a friend, even when I didn't want to admit it myself.

Now, 14 years later, we aren't just friends; we're sisters. Through the years, there have been countless late-night talks, tears shed, and laughs shared between us. I can't imagine what my life would be like without a Christian friend like that walking with me through it all. God has used her in my life in huge ways and still does to this day.

And that's the beauty of true friendship—especially the kind that forms when you least expect it. In those moments when you feel like you're drowning, having someone who genuinely cares can be the lifeline you never knew you needed. Sometimes, God's grace comes wrapped in the form of a friend who won't let you walk alone, no matter how much you try to convince yourself that you're fine on your own.

**Real-Life Application**

1. Do you truly allow other Christians to support and encourage you?

__________________________________________________

__________________________________________________

__________________________________________________

__________________________________________________

2.  Have you taken steps to build a community of fellow
    believers around you?

_______________________________________________

_______________________________________________

_______________________________________________

_______________________________________________

# Chapter 13 - Because of Your Goodness to Me: Reflecting on God's Faithfulness

*...because of your goodness to me. Psalm 142:7d*

The very end of David's prayer is a profound acknowledgment of God's unwavering faithfulness. Despite the trials and tribulations, he recognized and proclaimed God's goodness. Reflecting on God's faithfulness, especially during difficult times, is a powerful practice that can transform your perspective and refresh your heart.

When you face your own struggles, it can be easy to lose sight of God's goodness. Depression, anxiety, and life's pressures can cloud your mind, making it difficult to remember how God has been faithful in the past. However, reflecting on God's goodness is crucial for maintaining your faith and finding strength in adversity.

However, this reflection involves intentionally recalling and meditating on the ways Jesus has worked in your life. Here are some practical steps to help you cultivate this practice:

**Keep a Gratitude Journal:** Regularly write down instances of God's goodness in your life. These can be answered prayers, moments of comfort, acts of provision, or times when you felt His presence. Over time, this journal will become a powerful reminder of His faithfulness.

**Meditate on Scripture:** The Bible is filled with accounts of God's faithfulness. Passages like Lamentations 3:22-23, "Because of the Lord's great love we are not consumed, for his compassions never fail. They are new every morning; great is your faithfulness," can anchor you in God's promises.

**Share Testimonies:** Talking about God's goodness with others strengthens your faith and encourages those around you. Share your stories of His faithfulness in small groups, with friends, or during church gatherings.

**Reflect in Prayer:** Spend time in prayer, specifically thanking God for His goodness. Reflect on His faithfulness in your life and express your gratitude. This practice not only honors God but also shifts your focus from your problems to His providence.

**Celebrate Milestones:** Mark significant moments in your life where you experienced God's goodness. Whether it's a spiritual anniversary, a healing, or a breakthrough, celebrate these milestones as reminders of His faithfulness.

Reflecting on God's goodness can also bring healing and hope. In my own life, there were times when depression made it hard to see anything good. However, when I took the time to recall God's past faithfulness, I found renewed strength and hope. Remembering how He had been with me in previous struggles reassured me that He would not abandon me in my current situation.

David's practice of reflecting on God's goodness was not just a personal exercise but a declaration to others. By proclaiming God's faithfulness, he invited others to trust in the same steadfast God. Your reflections and testimonies can have a similar impact, encouraging those around you to see and trust in God's goodness.

The practice of reflecting on God's goodness also deepens your relationship with Him. It fosters a heart of gratitude, which is essential for spiritual growth. Gratitude shifts your focus from what you lack to what you have received, cultivating a positive outlook and a resilient spirit.

In conclusion, by regularly reflecting on God's goodness, you reinforce your trust in His promises and find the strength to endure life's challenges. David's example teaches us that no matter how dark the cave is, the light of God's faithfulness can shine through, guiding us toward hope and peace. Embrace this practice and let the remembrance of God's goodness transform your heart and renew your faith.

# True Story

Over the span of three nights, I found myself trapped in a recurring series of nightmares. The first night, I dreamt that my mom was coming to visit me. On her way, she got into a car accident and died. This nightmare replayed itself the following night, robbing me of hours of precious sleep. By the third night, the nightmare had evolved. A close friend, upon hearing about my mom's death, picked me up to take me somewhere. But we, too, got into a car accident, and she died as well.

Each nightmare was so vivid that I woke up drenched in sweat, tears streaming down my face, and my heart pounding as I reminded myself it wasn't real. The combination of losing sleep, battling turbulent emotions, and trying to keep up with college life left my mind in a constant fog. Talking to a counselor helped, but it didn't take away the deep sense of dread and despair that loomed over me. One night, as negative thoughts began to creep in, I could feel myself slowly sinking into depression.

In that moment of darkness, I remembered a piece of advice someone had given me during a rough time: make a list of three things you're grateful for each day for a month without repeating any. Desperate for relief, I decided to give it a try.

The first time I sat down to write my three things, it was simple. I jotted down the basics: my health, my family, my friends. After about a week, it started to get harder. I found myself staring at the paper, struggling to come up with anything new. Two weeks in, I was really pushing myself to find gratitude in the smallest of things. However, each day, despite the difficulty, I persevered.

I began to notice the little blessings around me—a hot cup of coffee on a cold morning, the beauty of a sunset, the sound of birds chirping outside my window. Slowly but surely, my perspective began to shift. The nightmares that once gripped my nights lost their power over me. The fog started to lift, and I could see a little more clearly.

It wasn't an instant transformation, but it was a steady one. This simple act of gratitude helped me to see the glimmers of light in the darkness. It reminded me that even in the midst of despair, there are always things to be thankful for. And with that realization came a newfound strength to keep moving forward, one day at a time.

1.  How often do you think about all God has done for
    you?

    _______________________________________

    _______________________________________

    _______________________________________

    _______________________________________

2.  What's one thing from this chapter you can start doing?

    _______________________________________

    _______________________________________

    _______________________________________

    _______________________________________